THE UNBEATABLE
MARTIN BRODEUR

ANDREW PODNIEKS

D0870403

Fenn Publishing Company Ltd.
Bolton, Canada

Fenn Publishing Company Ltd.

THE UNBEATABLE MARTIN BRODEUR

A Fenn Publishing Book / First Published in 2008

We acknowledge the financial support of the Government of Canada through the Book Publishing Industry Development Program (BPIDP) for our publishing activities This book is licensed by Hockey Canada.

Hockey Canada and the Hockey Canada logo are registered trademarks and may not be reproduced without the prior written consent of Hockey Canada.

Designed by First Image
Fenn Publishing Company Ltd.
Bolton, Ontario, Canada
Printed in Canada

Library and Archives Canada Cataloguing in Publication

Podnieks, Andrew, 1962-
The unbeatable Martin Brodeur / Andrew Podnieks.

ISBN 978-1-55168-346-1

1. Brodeur, Martin, 1972-. 2. Hockey goalkeepers--Canada--Biography.
3. Hockey goalkeepers--United States--Biography. I. Title.

GV848.5.B76B34 2008   J BIOGRAPH 796.962092   C2008-902079-0

THE UNBEATABLE · CANADA · MARTIN BRODEUR

CONTENTS

INTRODUCTION

"Playing for Canada and
winning an Olympic gold medal
is a dream."
Martin

When I was a kid, my friends and I used to play road hockey outside our house all the time in the winter and summer. Those were happy days when hockey was simple and fun, and that's the way I've tried to approach every game ever since, even though I've played in the NHL, a very serious league, all my adult life.

It's because of those memories that I brought the Stanley Cup home to my dad's house to play a road hockey game after winning the Stanley Cup with New Jersey. I've been fortunate enough to win three times, and my family, friends, and I have had three amazing road hockey games as a result.

I was always a goalie, and growing up my favourite team was, of course, the Montreal Canadiens. I admired Patrick Roy when he took the team to a surprise Cup win in 1986, and I later admired Ron Hextall because of the way he handled the puck. I tried to play a little bit like both of those great goalies, but I also tried to create my own style in goal.

It has worked well for me, and I am now very near two major records that many people thought would be impossible to beat—Terry Sawchuk's 103 regular-season shutouts and Patrick Roy's 551 career regular season wins. These were records I could never dream of beating when I played my first NHL game, but I've been fortunate enough to play on a very good team, stay healthy, and play at a consistently high level, something I'm very proud of.

For me, though, records aren't everything. I love to win, and I love it when my teammates and I shut out our opponents, but I also take pride in the way I play the game. Sportsmanship, fair play, and honour are qualities that are as important to me as any great save or big win. Sure, I want to win as badly as anyone else, but I want to win fair and square.

◀ *Denis Brodeur and two of his children, Martin (middle) and Denis, Jr.*

The first time Martin was on skates, and father Denis was there with his camera to capture the moment!

This book captures the essence of my career, starting with my childhood in St. Léonard, a small area just outside Montreal, to my years in junior hockey, and finally realizing my dream of playing in the NHL. It also shows how important international play is to me. Although I love winning the Stanley Cup, playing for Canada and winning an Olympic gold medal is a dream every bit as important to me. I guess that's in part because my dad played at the Olympics, and because as a kid I followed Team Canada like most other kids in the country. I also love the book's title—*The Unbeatable Martin Brodeur*! Okay, it's not true all the time, but I'd like to think that it's true most of the time! Enjoy.

Martin Brodeur

◄ *Martin as a teenager with St. Hyacinthe and his father, both goalies displaying the masks they wore during their time in goal.*

FOREWORD

Martin's father was also a
goalie as a kid, and he later
played in the Olympics.

In order to understand Martin Brodeur's incredible rise to become the number-one goalie in the world, it is important to start at a time well before Martin was even born. You see, back in 1956, Martin's father, Denis, was also a goaltender, good enough, in fact, to play for Canada at the Olympics nearly half a century before Martin did!

In the mid-1950s, Denis Brodeur played for a team called the Kitchener-Waterloo Dutchmen. This was an amateur hockey team, meaning that players got paid only a few dollars a week. They held other jobs during the day and played hockey, for the love of the game, at night. The K-W Dutchies, as they were known, were good enough to qualify to represent Canada at the 1956 Olympics in Cortina d'Ampezzo, Italy. This was at a time when only amateur athletes were eligible to compete at the Olympics, so no NHLers were allowed to represent their countries.

Denis and partner Keith Woodall shared the goaltending duties for Canada. Denis played the first game, and just like Martin would do many times, years later, Denis earned a shutout. Canada beat Germany, 4-0. In the next game, Keith was the goalie against a very weak team representing Austria, and Canada won easily, 23-0.

Denis then played in goal for the next three games, which were considered the most important games of the tournament for Canada. The Dutchies beat the host nation, Italy, by a slim 3-1 score and then faced a very skilled team from Czechoslovakia (the country later split in two sections called Czech Republic and Slovakia). The Czechs scored the first goal, but by the end of the first period Canada had tied the game. The Czechs scored early in the second to go up 2-1, but then the Dutchies scored three goals to take control. Canada won the game, 6-3, setting up a showdown against the United States.

◀ *Young Denis Brodeur was a goalie long before Martin entered the world.*

Denis Brodeur as a young man during his playing days with the Kitchener-Waterloo Dutchmen in the mid-1950s.

There was a problem in this game, though. All of the games in 1956 were still played outside, and in the first period Denis played facing directly into the lights of the arena for the afternoon game. John Mayasich, an American forward, lifted a high shot in from centre, and Denis couldn't see the puck to make the stop. In bounced in, and the U.S. went on to win the game, 4-1. Canada later beat Germany again, and then Sweden, but lost 2-0 to the Soviet Union in the final game of the round-robin schedule. The Dutchies finished in third place, good enough for the bronze medal but disappointing all the same.

Many years later, Denis Brodeur would be watching his own son play at the Olympics in Italy, in 2006, but the journey of Denis and Martin Brodeur inbetween those 50 years was one that made hockey history.

Denis Brodeur makes a save against Czechoslovakia at the 1956 Olympics as teammate Jack MacKenzie takes his man.

A BOY IN MONTREAL

CHAPTER ONE

"My coach came up to me and asked, 'Do you want to be a goalie or forward?'"

Martin

When Denis Brodeur was a small boy, he loved playing hockey in the winter and baseball in the summer. In hockey, he started skating and playing as a forward, but when he was about 16 years old he moved back into the crease and became a goalie. Incredibly, Denis was able to make the adjustment very quickly, and he was so good that within two years he was playing Junior B hockey in Champetre, a small region just north of Montreal. The next year he played briefly with Victoriaville. Coincidentally, one of his teammates was the great Jean Béliveau, and the two were teammates the next summer when both played baseball.

But hockey was Denis' true love, and he played goal for many more years. The trouble was that there were only six teams in the NHL in the 1950s (Toronto, Montreal, Boston, Chicago, Detroit, and New York Rangers), and that meant only six goalies were needed in the best league. Denis had to play in lower leagues, but this led him to Kitchener where he ended up helping his team win the Allan Cup, which in those days was as important as the Stanley Cup. The Allan Cup was for amateur teams and leagues (as opposed to professional NHL teams which competed for the Stanley Cup), and the Kitchener-Waterloo Dutchmen were the best in all of Canada in 1954-55. As a result, the team was asked to represent Canada at the 1956 Olympics.

Later that year, Denis married his girlfriend, Mireille, and in the ensuing years the happy couple had a big family. By the time Martin was born in 1972, there were four other siblings— oldest brother Claude; his other older brother, Denis Jr.; and, sisters Line and Sylvie. Martin grew up in a very athletic family and was always surrounded by sports in one way or another.

After Denis had retired as a goalie, he began a career as a sports photographer. He was very successful, and pretty soon he

◀ *Martin's enthusiasm for playing goal was evident early on and has always been an important part of why he plays the game.*

was the official photographer of the Montreal Canadiens. This meant he took the team picture at the start of the year, game action pictures from every game at the Forum in Montreal during the season, and often Stanley Cup photos at the end of the year. Denis was at the Forum pretty much every day during the season.

One of Martin's first memories was when he was three years old. His father took him and his two brothers to the Forum, an experience that helped shape Martin's love for hockey. Each year, the Canadiens invited journalists and photographers to the Forum to skate around the ice with their families. Father Denis took his kids and gave them a magical moment. "Everyone put on their skates," Martin remembered, "and around we went. For a kid, it was just, 'Wow!' Little things like that made me interested in hockey almost before I could walk. I began playing organized hockey at around four years old."

Like his father, Martin first played hockey as a skater, not a goalie. The family lived in a part of Montreal called St. Léonard, on Mauriac Street, and just down the road was Hébert Arena. Martin played for two teams in his first year of organized hockey. For his main team he was a forward, but for the other team made up of older boys, he was the backup goalie. As Martin explains, how he got on the second team is in part because of his brother, Denis Jr.. The rest, as they say, was history.

"I was the best player on my team when I was six," Martin began. "We were playing against teams in other cities. At the time, there was a team with older guys, including my brother [Denis], that was going to this tournament. They asked me to be the backup goalie, and I said sure. The next season, my coach came up to me and asked, 'Do you want to be a goalie or forward this year?' It was the biggest decision of my life, and I was seven years old. I don't know why I decided, but I thought it would be fun to play goal."

Fate had decided what Martin was going to do with the rest of his sporting life, although he didn't know it just yet. But his older brothers led the way. Claude, who was 13 years older, became an excellent baseball player and was a pitcher in the Montreal Expos farm system. Claude was also an excellent hockey player, but he decided to focus on baseball and gave up serious pursuit of the puck game. Denis loved bicycles and devoted his time to BMX riding. Martin was all about hockey, but he needed a little help from Claude at a critical time of his adolescence.

Martin loved playing hockey, but there was one incident that made him so upset he almost quit the game. It happened when he was 14 and playing bantam AA hockey. He had a game one night, but earlier in the day his grandmother had passed away, so he had to miss the game. When he returned to the team for its next game, the coach benched him. He benched Martin for three straight games, and Martin was so upset he wanted to quit. But Claude set him straight and took him to the next game himself. "He said to me, 'Hey, you go back, suck it up for a little bit. You never know what's going to happen,'" Martin explained. "It's weird, but if he never said anything then, I would probably not be playing hockey today."

> *"I don't know why I decided, but I thought it would be fun to play goal."*

Indeed, Martin's perseverance paid off. He continued to play goal, and a year later he was invited to try out for the under-16 Team Quebec. Martin earned the assignment as starting goalie and used that experience to play AAA in midget hockey. "Scouts from junior were at every game," he recalled. "They were all over me, and I had about 12 offers to universities in the States."

One of the reasons Martin had become so good was that even when he was four and five years old he would go to games and practices at the Forum with his father. Of course, the Montreal Canadiens became his favourite team, but more important, Martin got to watch NHL hockey up close. He could

Martin plays goal using his father's left-handed glove.

focus on a player and watch his every move, learn how the player acts and reacts during the pressure and action of a game. It was like Martin was in a video game, except everything he saw was live, up close, and very real!

During this critical time of his development both as a goalie and a young man, Martin began to consider hockey his life calling. In this respect, there were two parts of his life, two parts of his brain working together in his development as a goalie. First, there was his own playing, and second there was his up-close learning at the Forum.

His Montreal Bourassa AAA team played at the St. Léonard Arena, and it was there he became friends with the manager, Mario Baril. Mario was not just the manager of the arena; he was also a goalie coach, and every Saturday morning he held a clinic which Martin attended without fail. Mario taught Martin not only various styles of goaltending but psychological aspects of the game as well.

When he was four and five years old he would go to games and practices at the Forum with his father.

For instance, Mario pointed out that the best thing for a goalie to do is whatever confuses the shooter. If the shooter doesn't know what the goalie is going to do, he isn't as likely to score. Martin had been a standup goalie, meaning he waited for the player to shoot before deciding how to make a save. But at this time, the mid- to late-1980s, "butterfly" goalies were the most common. Their style was to go down as a player was shooting and make sure their pads were spread apart so that each skate was against a post.

But Mario told Martin that although both styles were good, both were predictable. Mario wanted Martin to do a bit of both. Don't be predictable. The two got along well, and Mario quickly became Martin's personal goalie coach. What is funny, and important, is that Martin's father almost never showed Martin

anything about playing the position. Denis wanted to be a supportive father, not a coach or a bossy dad, and that was fine for both father and son.

At this exact time, when Martin was learning how to play goal, he was also going to the Forum every chance he got. And in the 1985-86 season, that meant he got to watch a 20-year-old phenom named Patrick Roy play just about every night. "When Roy came in and made that stretch run and won the Cup and the Conn Smythe Trophy, I started saying, 'Wow. This is for real. Maybe I can do that,'" Martin admitted. "Til then, all of the goalies seemed old, you know, like veterans. You watched them, and you couldn't believe they stopped the kinds of shots they did. I was just a kid, and I couldn't imagine I'd ever be able to do that. Then, suddenly, there was Patrick Roy. He was a young guy from Quebec—like me. I idolized him because he came in so young, and he showed me he could do the job. He made me see the possibility of doing it myself."

> *"I idolized him because he came in so young, and he showed me he could do the job."*

Of course, Martin watched how Patrick made saves, how he went down but controlled his body position, how he got up quickly, always blocking as much of the net as possible. A year later, Martin became obsessed with a second goalie. Another young star in Philadelphia named Ron Hextall was making quite an impression in his first year in the NHL, and Martin watched him closely, too, but for different reasons.

Ron was quickly becoming famous for the way he handled the puck. He would skate into the corners to get it, rather than wait for it to roll behind the goal, and he would fire passes half the length of the ice sometimes. On penalty kills, Ron would ice the puck on his own, and sometimes his own players at centre ice would pass the puck back to him if they were in danger of losing it. Martin loved

◀ *Martin has a great seat in the house before a Montreal Canadiens home game, watching the warmup from the players' bench.*

Martin plays goal for his Montreal Bourassa midget team in 1988.

The Unbeatable Martin Brodeur

this creative playing. Ron became known as a "third defenceman," and Martin envisioned doing the same thing himself.

By playing and observing, by being coached and understanding the position, Martin was developing important skills for becoming the best he could be. He wanted to cover the lower half of the net using the butterfly style, but he wanted to stand up as much as possible because he also used the pokecheck and he wanted to be able to skate out of his crease to handle the puck whenever the opportunity arose. He wanted to take the best parts of all great goalies and put them into one new style of goaltending that was effective physically and most challenging for shooters.

By the time the summer of 1989 arrived, Martin was at a critical stage of his life. He was 17 years old and could envision himself playing hockey as a career, though had a major decision to make—whether to play university hockey in the United States, where he could also get an education while playing a good but not fantastic level of hockey, or play junior in Quebec, where the focus would be on the ice at all times. For Martin, the decision was easy. He stayed at home and played major junior hockey.

For Martin, the decision was easy. He stayed at home and decided to play major junior hockey.

Martin was selected by the Montreal Junior Canadiens in the Midget Draft, a team famous in the late 1960s for developing so many of the great Canadiens who won six Stanley Cups in the NHL during the 1970s. But, before the start of the 1989-90 season, the team moved and became known as the St. Hyacinthe Laser. It was at this time Martin had made a life decision he couldn't go back on soon. He wanted to be a goalie in the NHL, and he was now prepared to devote his life to pursuing this dream.

JUNIOR AND THE NHL SURPRISE

CHAPTER TWO

"I never thought of any career other than hockey."

Martin

I t was simple for Martin. "I never thought of any career other than hockey," he said. That's why choosing junior hockey over university was easy for him. "I think that's the only way I could have made it happen. No way out. No turning back. That's how I want things when I play."

It was a wise course of action for Martin for several reasons. He arrived at St. Hyacinthe's training camp and promptly impressed coach Norman Flynn, and it wasn't too long into camp before Martin and Yanick Degrace were the clear favourites to make the team. As it turned out, they more or less split the playing time during the season, although Martin played 42 games and Yanick 34. Martin was in goal for 23 of the team's 35 wins, and even though he was giving up four goals a game he was gaining tremendous experience and was still only 17 years old. By the end of the first season, Martin had become the team's top goalie, and he played every minute for the Laser in the 1990 playoffs.

That summer of 1990 was exciting for Martin. He was now 18 years old, and this meant he was eligible for the NHL Entry Draft. He would definitely be selected, the only questions were by which team and at what point in the draft process.

The draft that year was held at BC Place in Vancouver, and Martin didn't have to wait long to hear his name called. It was a strange and ominous day all the same. Calgary owned the 20th overall selection but the Flames wanted to select a particular goalie and traded with New Jersey to move up to the 11th position. The Flames then chose Trevor Kidd, and in 20th position the New Jersey Devils took Martin Brodeur.

This was the one of several connections between the two goalies, Martin and Trevor. During the previous season, Trevor, who played in the Western Hockey League (WHL) for the Brandon Wheat Kings, was invited to tryouts for Team Canada at the World Junior Championship, to be held that year in

◄ *Martin gets an encouraging pat from Soviet goaltending great Vladislav Tretiak.*

Martin makes a glove save in junior with the St. Hyacinthe Laser.

Saskatoon, Saskatchewan. Martin was not invited. Trevor made the team as the backup goalie, but he didn't play a game.

The next year, after both players had been drafted, Trevor was again invited to Canada's World Junior camp and Martin wasn't, and Trevor was the number-one goalie for Canada that year. The year after, for the 1992 World Junior Championship, Martin was finally invited, but he was cut from the team. Trevor was again the starting goalie, playing the entire tournament for Canada.

Perhaps those decisions were right at the time based on how the two goalies were playing, but anyone can see looking back that Martin's career only got greater and greater while Trevor's reached its peak at the WJC and never really took off once he got to the NHL. Trevor played for four teams over a 13-year period and a total of only 387 games.

After being drafted, Martin knew more than ever he was on track to make the NHL, so he returned to St. Hyacinthe for the 1990-91 season with added confidence. He was a year older and a year more experienced, and he knew where he was going in the long term. He was clearly the team's number-one goalie now ahead of backup Stephane Menard, and he was looking at this season as the first real step toward the NHL.

He was clearly learning more and more with every game he played.

Martin won only 22 of 52 games with the Laser that year, though, but the team was not one of the best in the QMJHL. Still, his GAA of 3.30 was among the league leaders, and he was clearly learning more and more with every game he played. He had one more year left to play with the Laser, and New Jersey was in no rush to bring him to the NHL before he was fully mature physically and fully prepared mentally.

As a result, Martin considered the next year, 1991-92, his last in junior. After that, he was going to be a pro, either with the Devils or with their minor-league affiliate in Utica, New York. He was still the number-one goalie with the Laser, but in addition to Stephane Menard there was also a third goalie, J.F. Rivard, who also played a few games.

Late in that season, Martin's life changed forever. The New Jersey Devils were in desperate need of a goalie for their game the night of March 26, 1992. Their top two goalies, Chris Terreri and Craig Billington, were both injured, so the team called Martin up on an emergency basis. This meant he could only play until one of the regular New Jersey goalies was healthy again, at which point the Devils would have to return Martin to junior. Martin's dream was now a reality. He quickly called his parents and a few friends, and they drove from Montreal to New Jersey in time for the opening faceoff.

"Do I remember that first game?" Martin asked with a smile. "Monday I was in juniors; Thursday night I was playing against the Boston Bruins. I was 19, and I couldn't stop a puck in warm-up. The coaches came up to me and said, 'Don't worry, kid. Just go out there and have fun.' So I did. The first shot I stopped was a long one by Don Sweeney. We won the game, 4-2."

> "Monday
> I was in juniors;
> Thursday night
> I was playing
> against the
> Boston Bruins."

And that's how Martin Brodeur made it to the NHL. He played his second game two nights later, again allowing just two goals in a 5-2 win over the Quebec Nordiques. The next night he was the backup to Craig Billington, but Craig wasn't fully recovered and Martin played the second and third periods. Philadelphia won that game, 5-4, and Martin allowed all five goals. He was sent back to St. Hyacinthe, but a couple of weeks later he was back for one game. Again he was the backup as Chris Terreri started, but Chris allowed five goals in two periods and Martin played the third period of a 7-0 loss to the New York Islanders.

The Unbeatable Martin Brodeur

Martin (left) with Stephane Fiset (middle) and Felix Potvin at the QMJHL All-Star Game in 1990.

Martin makes a save in the minors, with the Utica Devils of the AHL.

Martin makes a save against Boston as Steve Heinze follows the play. It was Martin's first NHL game and he wore number 29.

The Laser were eliminated in the first round of the playoffs, so Martin was able to spend some of the playoffs with the Devils. At this stage of his career, every bit of NHL experience was important even if it meant watching from the players' bench as a backup or from the press box as a healthy scratch.

Nevertheless, he appeared in his first playoff game on April 27, 1992, when he again replaced Chris Terreri in a game against the New York Rangers. Chris allowed five goals in just 28 minutes, and Martin allowed three more in 32 minutes of an 8-5 loss. It would be a while before Martin would see the NHL again, but the 1991-92 season was huge for his confidence and enthusiasm. He had tasted life in the NHL, and now, more than ever, he wanted to feast on it.

In just his second career game, Martin stops Quebec Nordiques' young star Mats Sundin from in close.

FAST LEARNER

CHAPTER THREE

It was only his eighth career NHL game, and Martin already had his first shutout.

But before a return to the NHL, Martin had to be patient. He played all of 1992-93 in the minors. He was too good to stay in junior any longer, but the Devils felt he wasn't just ready yet for the daily demands of the NHL. A year in the minors was a great transition for him, they felt. General Manager Lou Lamoriello told Martin as much, and this helped Martin overcome any disappointment he might have felt. Lou knew that Martin was the team's goalie of the future, and he wanted Martin to play one year in the minors no matter what.

Actually, the year started badly for Martin after he suffered a knee injury near the beginning of the season that required minor surgery. But he came back healthy and strong, and in Utica he shared the goaltending duties with Corey Schwab. Both goalies played well for coach Robbie Ftorek, but Martin played all of the playoffs for the AHL Devils. This turned out to be for only one round as the team was eliminated in a five-game series against the Rochester Americans.

The connection between a minor-league team and its NHL affiliate is important because the AHL is where many players develop the skills needed to become top NHLers. For Martin, he had played well in his first year of pro with Utica, but he needed a little luck to make it to New Jersey the next year. And if luck was what he needed, luck was what he got!

At training camp in 1993 with New Jersey, Martin was the third-ranked goalie behind Chris Terreri and Peter Sidorkiewicz. This meant he was likely going to be sent back to Utica at the end of training camp. But then Peter suffered an injury to his

◀ *Martin stops Stu Barnes of Dallas simply through excellent positioning.*

Fast Learner

Uncorking his trademark clearing pass, Martin moves the puck up ice quickly.

shoulder, and on opening night Martin was the backup goalie to Chris. The next game, however, on the road in Washington, coach Jacques Lemaire decided to give Martin the start. Martin stopped 23 of 26 shots and the Devils beat the Capitals, 6-3, and the goalie's confidence grew a little more.

Jacques Lemaire was coaching New Jersey for the first time, taking over from Herb Brooks, and as part of his new staff he brought in Jacques Caron as a goalie coach. This was great for Martin because the two had worked together in Utica. Jacques knew what kind of a goalie Martin was, and he knew the kinds of things they had to practice.

Coach Lemaire decided to alternate Chris and Martin at the start of the season, and so each goalie would play every other game. Martin won his next start a few nights later, beating Winnipeg, 7-4, and then a week later he won for the third time in a row, this a 4-0 decision over Anaheim. It was only his eighth career NHL game, and Martin already had his first shutout. It was to be his first of three that year, and the first of many during his career.

> *By early December, it was clear Martin had already made the adjustment to the NHL.*

By early December, it was clear Martin had already made the adjustment to the NHL, and for the rest of the season he became the number-one goalie. Chris Terreri still played quite a bit as well, but Martin played against the tougher teams and being eight years younger than Chris he knew he was the goalie of the future for New Jersey.

The Devils were leading the league in goals against at Christmas, and Martin got better and better as the season went on. By the time the 84-game regular season was over, Martin had won 27 of 47 games in which he appeared and had a sparkling 2.40 GAA. For his great rookie season he won the Calder Trophy, beating out Edmonton's Jason Arnott (a future teammate of Martin with the Devils) and Philadelphia's Mikael Renberg.

The Devils finished with a team record 106 points and were playing with confidence heading into the playoffs. They beat the Buffalo Sabres in a thrilling seven-game series in the first round, and Martin played most of the games. The next round, against Boston, saw Chris and Martin share the games, and again the Devils won the series, eliminating the Bruins in six games.

Even though he was mad at himself for allowing the goal, he couldn't let that one goal disrupt his entire career.

The Conference finals were against rivals New York Rangers, and this turned out to be a classic confrontation. It went seven games, and Martin played almost every minute of the entire series. But the Rangers, led by captain Mark Messier, won 2-1 in double overtime of game seven. It was a heartbreaking loss because the winning goal was scored by Stephane Matteau on a wraparound, the kind of play a goalie is expected to stop every time. The Rangers went on to win the Stanley Cup for the first time since 1940.

Martin did what any great player has to do in a situation like this, though. He controlled his emotions. Even though he was mad at himself for allowing the goal, he couldn't let that one goal disrupt his entire career. He was able to look back at the season as a whole, and he was incredibly satisfied. He was 22 years old. He had finished his first season in the NHL and won the Calder Trophy. And he was clearly the goalie the Devils wanted to rely on for many years to come. One goal could not ruin those accomplishments.

The Unbeatable Martin Brodeur

Martin won the Calder Trophy as the NHL's rookie of the year at the end of the 1993-94 season.

BRODEUR THE UNSTOPPABLE

"Every night of our childhood we would play street hockey."

Martin

Martin came to New Jersey's training camp to begin the 1994-95 season feeling on top of the world. He was ready to take charge in goal and become one of the best goalies in the league. There was a big problem, though. The players and the NHL were in a fight over a new contract, and so the start of the season was delayed one week, two weeks, one month, and on until January 1995. By the time a new deal was agreed to, there was time to play only a 48-game season and then the full schedule of playoff games.

No matter to Martin. Although Chris Terreri was still the Devils' other goalie, Martin played in 40 of the 48 games and was sensational. The Devils finished only third in the Atlantic Division with 52 points, but the team felt confident heading into the playoffs again. In the first round, they easily beat Boston in just five games, a feat made special because Martin tied an all-time NHL record by recording three shutouts in that one series. In the next round they beat the Pittsburgh Penguins also in five games. In the Conference finals they played the Flyers, and this was a strange series because the road team won all of the first five games.

New Jersey won the first two games in Philadelphia, then the Flyers won the next two at the Meadowlands Arena, but New Jersey won the next two games to eliminate the Flyers and advance to the Stanley Cup finals. A team only a few years earlier dubbed as a "Mickey Mouse" club by Wayne Gretzky—because it was so weak—was now set to play seven games for the greatest trophy in hockey.

New Jersey prepared to face the Detroit Red Wings in a seven-game series with the winner taking home the Stanley Cup. Martin had a great team in front of him with the two "great Scotts," defencemen Scott Stevens and Scott Niedermayer, and they had a group of scorers who contributed every night without relying on one star player. Detroit had goalies Chris Osgood and

◄ *Martin's steady and superior play quickly made him one of the best goalies in the league.*

Coming out to play the puck before his opponents can get to it,
Martin rifles the puck along the glass and around the boards.

Sometimes a goalie has to improvise, and here Martin goes from the left to the right to try to pokecheck an oncoming attacker.

Mike Vernon, and two great defencemen of their own, Nicklas Lidstrom and Slava Fetisov. They also had great strength up front led by captain Steve Yzerman and super Russian Sergei Fedorov. And, the team was coached by Scotty Bowman, who also coached in Montreal when New Jersey's coach, Jacques Lemaire, was still a player.

Yet in this series, it was the young guns from New Jersey who won. Martin played all but eight minutes of the entire series, and the Devils won the Stanley Cup in four straight games. The scores were 2-1, 4-2, 5-2, and 5-2. Martin had done just what Patrick Roy had done a few years earlier, and Martin knew that somewhere in the hockey world a small boy was watching him, being inspired by him, just as he was watching Patrick in Montreal in 1986.

By this time in Stanley Cup history, every player on the team was allowed to take the Stanley Cup home for one day in the summer, and Martin took this opportunity to take the Cup home to Mauriac Street, where he grew up and his parents still lived. This was the house that his parents bought after they got married in 1956, and it was the house they still lived in almost 40 years later. Recreating his childhood, Martin invited his friends over for a friendly game of road hockey, except this time the winning team got the Stanley Cup! "Every night of our childhood we would play street hockey," Martin said. "So, it's great to be able to come back and do the same thing and play for the real Stanley Cup."

Martin played out in that game while a friend played in goal, but guess what? Martin's road hockey team lost the game! No worries. Martin still had his name engraved on the Cup, and his place in history was now set even if he never played another NHL game in his life.

> *Martin played all but eight minutes of the entire series, and the Devils won the Stanley Cup in four straight games.*

◀ *After only two full seasons in the NHL, Martin led the Devils to the team's first Stanley Cup, in 1995.*

THE BEST IN THE GAME

CHAPTER FIVE

He fired it high in the air
in one motion, and the puck
landed in the empty net.

While Martin clearly asserted himself as the starting goalie in New Jersey during the 1994-95 season, he established himself as one of the best in the league the following season. He set an all-time NHL record by playing in 4,433 minutes during the season, and this came by appearing in 77 of the team's 82 games. During one stretch he started an amazing 44 straight games. Chris Terreri played in just four games, and a third goalie, Corey Schwab, made ten appearances.

Martin had a spectacular GAA of just 2.34 and was chosen the starting goalie for the Eastern Conference at the 1996 All-Star Game. He stopped all 12 shots he faced in the first period of the game, but the season was ultimately disappointing because the Devils failed to make the playoffs. They were in the tough Atlantic Division, and although they had a 37-33-12 record (Martin recording 34 of those 37 victories), they finished in sixth place.

The early end to the season allowed Martin the opportunity to play for Team Canada at the World Championship, though, and he teamed with Curtis Joseph to bring his country a silver medal. Prior to the start of the next season, he again was selected to play for Canada at the first World Cup of Hockey, again splitting the duties with Curtis.

The most important thing for Martin at this stage of his career was that he was developing his own style. He called it a "hybrid" style, meaning he combined certain aspects of many other styles. In truth, you could say he was a bit of Patrick Roy combined with a bit of Ron Hextall. That is, he liked to stay on

◀ *The rewards for a long year of play to win the Cup is a day relaxing with the great trophy in the summer.*

his feet so that he maintained good balance and could play the puck quickly. But he also learned how to go down and come up quickly, go from one post to the other to make saves off one-timers, and learned to have a disciplined body at all times. He didn't flop around like Dominik Hasek. Martin worked with coach Jacques Caron every day to perfect his style and to understand what was most successful in stopping shooters from scoring.

What Martin did better than any other goalie, though, was handle the puck. He not only did so in a defensive role but also to create offence. So, sometimes he raced out to get a shoot-in to play it to his defenceman quickly, but sometimes he looked up ice and fired a long pass to a forward hoping to catch the other team off-guard on a slow line change. He was the best in the league at this because every day in practice he worked on handling the puck and shooting it the length of the ice.

The truth was that one of the reasons Martin worked on playing the puck was that he had a dream of scoring a goal.

The truth was that one of the reasons Martin worked on playing the puck was that he had a dream of scoring a goal. He had seen Ron Hextall score twice by firing it the length of the ice near the end of a game with the other team pressing to tie the game and the goalie on the bench for the extra attacker. Martin had a simple rule. If he had an empty net and his team were winning by one goal, he would not try for a goal because if he missed there would be an icing call and that would give the opposition a faceoff in New Jersey's end. This might lead to a good chance to tie the game. But if the Devils had a two-goal lead, he felt this was enough of a lead to risk the play.

On April 17, 1997, Martin's dream came true. In a home playoff game against Montreal, his Devils were winning 4-2 late in the game. The Canadiens pulled their goalie, Jocelyn Thibault,

Martin (above, in red shorts) returned to his roots and played a road hockey game during his day with the Cup, the winning team receiving the great trophy.

Martin has played in nine All-Star Games so far during his career.

for a sixth attacker, setting the stage for Martin's shot. Montreal dumped the puck into the New Jersey end in the final minute to try to create some pressure, but Martin raced out to play the puck. He fired it high in the air in one motion, and the puck landed in the empty net. He started jumping up and down, unable to contain his excitement, unable to believe what he had just done.

The 1996-97 season was further important because Martin led the entire NHL with a 1.88 goals-against average to win his first Jennings Trophy. He did so while playing 67 games and winning 37 of those, including recording a league-best ten shutouts. He lost only 14 times, but the team didn't have as much success in the playoffs, losing to the New York Rangers in the Conference semi-finals. Martin was now among the very best goalies in the league and a goalie whose ability to handle the puck actually affected the way other teams played New Jersey. The rule was that when a team played Martin, it couldn't dump the puck in because Martin would shoot it out just as quickly.

All of his development was a terrific lead-in to the 1998 Olympics. For the first time in NHL history, the league was going to stop play for two and a half weeks to allow many of the players to participate in the Olympic Winter Games. Martin was excited when he was named to Team Canada, and even more excited to learn his roommate would be number 99, Wayne Gretzky, but his experience in Nagano, Japan wasn't as he had expected. The other goalie was none other than Patrick Roy, who had never before been selected to play for Canada at any level. Patrick was named the top goalie, but he also insisted on playing in all the games in Japan, meaning Martin could only watch from the bench. It was not a "team first" move by Patrick, but Martin learned from the trip all the same.

Patrick may have been a great NHL goalie, but he was not able to take his best game to the international arena. He was outplayed by Czech goalie Dominik Hasek in a shootout in the semi-finals, and then in the bronze medal game he put in a weak performance and Canada had to settle for a very disappointing fourth place. Still, just being part of the Olympics gave Martin a clear goal for 2002—to be Canada's starting goalie.

Martin returned to New Jersey and put in his best season yet. He played in 70 more games and led the league with 43 wins, the first of four straight seasons in which he was number one in this statistic. His next three seasons were much the same, but it was the last of these, 1999-2000, that Martin made it back to the Stanley Cup finals.

In fact, Martin was sensational in the 2000 playoffs. He played every minute of the post-season after recording 43 of the team's 45 regular-season victories. The Devils knocked off Florida in four games straight, Toronto in six games, and Philadelphia in seven games to reach the finals where they played Dallas, the defending Stanley Cup champions. Martin, however, was brilliant and outplayed Stars' goalie Ed Belfour, allowing only nine goals in a six-game series win. It was Martin's second Cup win and one more deserving than his first because it took place during a full season when the Devils were clearly one of the best teams in the league over a long schedule.

Earlier in the regular season, Martin was also credited with his second career goal.

Earlier in the regular season, Martin was also credited with his second career goal, and it turned out to be the game winner. Midway through the third period of a game against Philadelphia, the Devils were going to be called for a penalty, so the Flyers pulled their goalie since they kept possession of the puck. But after Martin made a save, Daymond Langkow of the Flyers tried to make a pass to a teammate. It was off the mark and slid all the way down the ice into the empty Philadelphia net! That made the score 3-1 New Jersey, and the Flyers later scored to make the final, 3-2. Martin got credit for the goal because he was the last New Jersey player to touch the puck before it entered

the net.

After winning the Cup in 2000, Martin again got to take the great trophy home for a day and again he hosted a road hockey game on the street of his childhood. He was also honoured when the local arena he had played in as a kid, the St. Léonard Arena, was re-named the Martin Brodeur Arena.

The next year was almost as perfect. Martin led the regular season with 42 wins, and he took the Devils to the finals again. Unfortunately, in 2001 they played Colorado, a team led by Joe Sakic and goalie Patrick Roy. Colorado won the first game, 5-0, but the Devils fought back to win three of the next four, setting up a game six battle in New Jersey with the Cup in the building ready for the Devils to claim. During the pre-game skate, though, teammate Colin White hit Martin in the head with a shot, and Martin never fully recovered that night. The Devils lost, 4-0, and now they had to go to Denver to play game seven.

> *Martin led the regular season with 42 wins, and he took the Devils to the finals again.*

The atmosphere in the Pepsi Center that night was electric, but that only helped the Avalanche. The Devils never got on track. Colorado won 3-1 to win the Cup, but it was really in game six at home that New Jersey lost the series. The season was a great one for Martin, though, and it set himself up perfectly for the 2001-02 season, another in which the NHL would shut down for two weeks for the Olympics in Salt Lake City, Utah.

Four years after Nagano, Martin was on the team and Patrick wasn't, but Martin was feeling a bit on the outside again because Canada's other goalie was Curtis Joseph. The Team Canada coach was Pat Quinn, Curtis's NHL coach in Toronto. Martin was worried that again he wouldn't be given priority because the coach would favour the goalie he knew better, and although he was right, everything worked out well in the end.

◀ *Martin with the Jennings Trophy in 1996-97,*
  his first of four so far.

CHAPTER SIX

CANADIAN GOLD

"We felt all along the expectations of all the people in Canada."

Martin

In the weeks leading up to the 2002 Olympics in Salt Lake City, Utah, Martin was feeling frustrated. Since the previous Olympics four years ago in Japan, he had been without doubt the best goalie in the NHL. But Curtis Joseph was playing really well in Toronto, and Team Canada's Olympic coach was Pat Quinn, who was also coach of the Maple Leafs.

Of course, a coach usually relies on players he knows well, so it was pretty obvious that coach Quinn would give the advantage to Curtis and not Martin. Martin hadn't played even one minute of the Olympics in Japan, and now he worried the same thing would happen to him all over again. Still, he decided to put his worries in the back of his mind and go to Salt Lake City with only positive thoughts.

Patrick Roy did just the opposite. He was the man in 1998 who played every minute for Team Canada when the national team failed to win a medal. This was the only time he ever played internationally for Canada, and now, in 2002, when he wasn't listed among the first eight players that every team had to name to the preliminary roster, he decided not to play. It was a selfish decision based on ego, and just the opposite of the team-oriented decision by Martin to accept any role he might be given. After all, a player only has the chance to go to so many Olympics during his career, and Martin wasn't going to miss one for any reason.

Canada came to Salt Lake as the favourites to win gold. The team simply had no weakness. There was the general manager, Wayne Gretzky, and coach Pat Quinn. Martin and Curtis were the goalies. The defence included Scott Niedermayer, Rob Blake, and Ed Jovanovski. The forwards were led by captain

◀ In action during the gold-medal game of the 2002 Olympics, Martin follows play with John LeClair of Team USA in front.

Mario Lemieux as well as Jarome Iginla, Joe Sakic, Steve Yzerman, and Paul Kariya. In all, there were 12 certain hall of famers in the lineup.

As expected, though, game one saw Curtis Joseph in goal and Martin on the bench as his backup. Curtis was in the middle of an excellent three-year streak with the Maple Leafs and was having a phenomenal season. No one could deny that. And, Curtis and Martin had been in this position twice before—at the 1996 World Championship and the 1996 World Cup of Hockey. Both times Curtis was the number-one goalie and Martin the backup. Both times Canada failed to win gold. Who could blame Martin, who had won the Stanley Cup with New Jersey in 1995 and 2000, for feeling a little frustrated? Curtis had never won a Cup or a gold medal.

Canada came to Salt Lake as the favourites to win gold. The team simply had no weakness.

Nevertheless, on the night of February 15, 2002, as Canada started the Olympics against Sweden, Curtis was in goal. There were other elements of the game that were important as well. Sweden's best player was Mats Sundin, a teammate of Curtis's in Toronto. Who would have the advantage? The goalie knew everything about the shooter's tendencies, but the shooter knew all about the goalie's weaknesses! On this night, it was no contest. Mats scored twice against Curtis, and the Swedes roared to a dominating 5-2 victory.

The setup for this Olympics was odd because the first three games of this preliminary round didn't count for very much. In other words, there were two groups of four teams each, and after each team played every other in the group, all eight nations advanced to an elimination quarter-finals game. This setup was put in place so that the teams, with so many NHL players, could have three games to play together and gel as a team without worrying about being sent home.

Martin tries to tend goal while Martin Rucinsky of the Czech Republic gets in his way during the 2002 Olympics.

Canada wins gold! Martin jumps for joy as the team wins Olympic gold for the first time in 50 years.

As a result, the 5-2 loss to Sweden was not a major worry in terms of getting to the gold-medal game, but it was a worry because Sweden had played so much better than Canada. The teams exchanged goals in the first period, but in the second period the Swedes scored four times to pull away. Pat Quinn was not willing to gamble on this same lineup for a second game, so when Canada played Germany two nights later, changes were made.

Most important, coach Quinn had decided to shake things up by putting Martin Brodeur in goal. This was a major decision for several reasons. First, although Martin was a star goalie in the NHL, he had yet to win a game in a Team Canada sweater. He was shut out in 1996 at both the World Championship and World Cup, and he didn't win at the 1997 World Championship either. In 1998, he didn't even get to play at the Olympics. Still, he was ready for anything and had already decided to play a more conservative game on the bigger international ice.

> Most important, coach Quinn had decided to shake things up by putting Martin Brodeur in goal.

"It's an exciting time," he said when he learned of coach Quinn's decision. "I'm going to stay a little deeper in my net and not challenge as much," he explained. Martin also made history once the puck was faced off to start the game. He and his father, Denis, became the first father and son tandem to play for Canada at the Olympics.

Canada played without captain Mario in that second game. He had a hip injury, and the team started without the usual confidence one can expect from a Canadian team. Although Canada had the edge in play, the first period was scoreless. The team erupted for three goals in the second, though, but the third was far more nerve-wracking than anyone in Canada had hoped for. Germany scored twice, the second goal bouncing off the butt end of Martin's stick and into the net. In fact, the Germans did everything but tie the game. Still, Martin and Canada won, setting up an important game against the Czech Republic.

Pat Quinn decided to go with Martin in goal again, and it was in this game that Martin earned his place as the starter for the rest of the Olympics. "I play every day in New Jersey," he said, "so I always have it in my mind that I'm going to play. I was happy to get the start. My first goal was to play in the Olympics. This is an opportunity, and I don't want to miss the boat."

He didn't. Both teams each scored one goal in each period, and the game ended in a 3-3 tie. But Martin made the save of the tournament early in the third period when he literally dove across the crease to make a blocker save on a one-timer and sure goal. The next day, Wayne Gretzky said, "it's highly unlikely there will be a change," when a reporter asked him about who would be the starting goalie for the next game, a quarter-finals showdown with Finland.

> *It was in this game that Martin earned his place as the starter for the rest of the Olympics.*

Indeed, Martin was in net, but Canada played a great game in front of him and the Finns were able to generate little offence. The result was a close but impressive 2-1 win for the Canadians. "They had a few opportunities to come at me," Martin explained in the media area after the game, "but I don't know what they were doing. They were making drop pass after drop pass. They weren't really shooting the puck that much." And when they did shoot, Martin was there to make the save.

The Canadians caught a break in the semi-finals. They were supposed to play Sweden, but the Swedes lost in the quarter-finals to Belarus, 4-3, and as a result it was Canada-Belarus playing for one spot in the gold-medal game. This was no contest, though, and Canada skated to an easy 7-1 win. Martin faced only 14 shots and the game was never in doubt.

The on-ice team portrait after players received their gold medals.

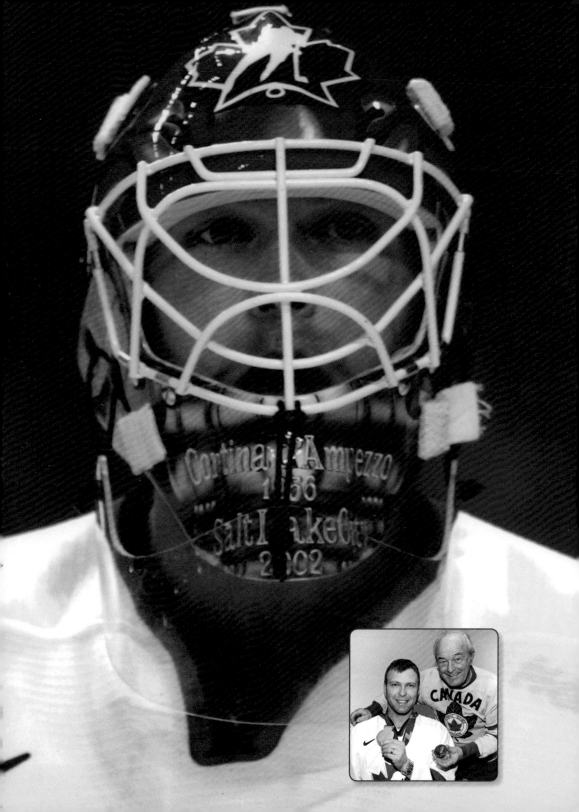

This meant that the championship was to be played two days later, Canada playing the host USA team that had arrived at the finals after a big 3-2 win over Russia. The last time these teams played a big game was the final game of the World Cup in 1996. Martin was on the bench and Curtis Joseph in goal, and the Americans won, 5-2. This time, Martin was the starting goalie and Curtis was on the bench.

The Americans scored first, but Martin had little chance on the play. The goal came during a 2-on-1, and Tony Amonte drilled a one-timer between Martin's legs as the goalie was going from side to side. Canada scored twice to take the lead after the first period, and most of the second was tense. The USA scored the tying goal late in the second, but Joe Sakic put Canada ahead again at 18:19. In the third period, 20 minutes to decide gold, Canada pulled away and Martin shut the door. Jarome Iginla and Joe Sakic scored again to make the final 5-2, and Canada was Olympic champions!

> "The gold medal is the only thing that makes people stop and want to touch it. That was a big turning point in my career."

"We were holding them off in the third period, and they made some great plays on the power play," Martin said afterwards, the gold medal around his neck. "When we got the fourth goal, it was a big moment, and we could see the end of the tunnel. We're excited. We felt all along the expectations of all the people in Canada. I'll always remember this."

Martin took his gold medal home to Montreal, and despite all the other great prizes he has won during his career, this stands out. "I've got my Stanley Cup rings and all my trophies at home," he said later, "but the gold medal is the only thing that makes people stop and want to touch it. That was a big turning point in my career." Indeed, it was.

◄ Martin's 2002 mask honours his own participation in the Olympics as well as his dad's play with Team Canada in 1956.

(inset) Father and son with their Olympic medals, Martin's gold and Denis' bronze.

BETWEEN OLYMPICS

CHAPTER SEVEN

It was clear Martin deserved to be the main goalie for Canada at the 2004 World Cup.

Martin returned to New Jersey with a gold medal around his neck, but although he had a strong finish to the season the Devils did not. They finished in third place in the Atlantic Division, just one point behind second-place New York Islanders and two points behind Philadelphia in top spot, but in the first round of the playoffs they faced Carolina, a young and hungry team with few players who had been to the Olympics. As a result, they were well rested while New Jersey, with many of their top players exhausted from a long season already, was not ready to challenge. The Hurricanes won the series in six games, and Martin went home early.

Nevertheless, Martin was entering the very prime of his career. At the end of the 2002-03 season he won his first Vézina Trophy as the league's outstanding goalie, and for good reason. He led the league with 41 wins and nine shutouts, and he played more than 70 games (73, to be exact) for the seventh time in his nine full seasons in the league. He was also named to the First All-Star Team for the first time, and, most important of all, he led the Devils to their third Stanley Cup in nine seasons.

Martin was almost unbeatable in the playoffs. He played in all 24 post-season games, won all 16 games needed to win the Cup, and set an all-time NHL record with seven shutouts. The Devils defeated Boston in five games in the opening round and Tampa Bay in five games in the next round. They eliminated Ottawa in a tense seven-game Conference finals to meet Anaheim for the Stanley Cup, a finals won in game seven when Martin posted a 3-0 shutout win. It was his record-tying third shutout of the series, and he became only the third goalie in NHL history to record a shutout in game 7 of the finals.

◀ *Down but not out, Martin tries to block as much of the net as possible to prevent a Colorado player from scoring.*

Martin's great play at the 2002 Olympics ensured he was the number-one goalie for the World Cup of Hockey two and a half years later.

Typical of Martin, though, it was a moment in game three against the Ducks that remains one of the memorable highlights of the year's playoffs. The Devils had won the first two games to take control of the series and they had tied game three 1-1 to give the Ducks a real scare. Then Martin made a crazy mistake. He came out to play the puck, but he lost control of his stick. Sandis Ozolinsh got to the puck and took a weak shot that hit the stick and bounced weakly into the net. Anaheim won the game, 3-2, in overtime to get right back in the series. For most other goalies, the play might have been devastating. Not for Martin.

"I was laughing at myself," he said after. "I was like, 'This is unbelievable. You're in the Stanley Cup final. You know how many millions of people are watching you, and your stick slips out of your hand and you get scored on. And they [teammates] were laughing at me." That was the character of the team. It was a silly goal at an important time, but they laughed it off. They knew Martin would recover. He did, and the Devils won the Cup.

It was a silly goal at an important time, but they laughed it off. They knew Martin would recover.

Although he won the Vézina Trophy a week later at the NHL Awards ceremony, Martin was denied the Conn Smythe Trophy. It was given instead to the man at the other end, the losing end, Anaheim's J-S Giguere. J-S had a great playoffs, to be sure, but Martin set records and won the final, all-important game, and many people felt the Conn Smythe should have been his rightful honour.

In 2003-04, Martin continued his brilliant play by leading the league again in games played (75), wins (38), minutes played (4,555), and shutouts (11). The team lost to Philadelphia in five games in the first round of the playoffs, though, a disappointing end to another 100-point regular season performance by the Devils. For Martin personally, though, he won the Vézina

Trophy for the second straight year, further solidifying his place as the best in the game.

Because of his play in Salt Lake for the 2002 Olympics, and his continued great play ever since, it was clear Martin deserved to be the main goalie for Canada at the 2004 World Cup of Hockey that September. Indeed, he was spectacular for Canada, winning the first four games by making great, timely saves. In the team's opening game against the United States, he stopped Tony Amonte cold while Amonte had already raised his arms, thinking that he'd scored. Tony simply didn't think it was possible that Martin could go from one post to the other to make the save. Not possible for most goalies, perhaps, but just another great save for the best goaltender in the world. In the next game, a 2-0 win over Russia, Alexander Frolov was stopped dead by Martin, angering the Russian to the point that he slammed his stick on the ice in a mixture of fury and frustration.

> *"The timely saves that I make, I think that's where it really hurts the teams I play against."*

Martin knew that at this world-class level, with this team, it wasn't how many shots he stopped so much as when he stopped them. "I know I'm playing for a great team," he said, "and I'm not going to get 50 shots on me. But the timely saves that I make, I think that's where it really hurts the teams I play against."

As coach Pat Quinn allowed: "He might now be the best in the game."

Canada's fourth game, a 5-0 win for Martin over Slovakia, produced some tense moments, though, because he took a shot off his wrist and didn't practice for a few days. However, x-rays revealed no broken bones, and Martin was back in goal for the championship game against Finland.

Martin holds the unique World Cup of Hockey championship trophy high as captain Mario Lemieux looks on.

Martin prepares for player introductions prior to the 2004 All-Star Game in Minnesota.

This tournament, however, was the last serious hockey anyone played for many months. A major disagreement between the NHL and NHL Players' Association saw the cancellation of the entire season, and for the first time since the influenza pandemic of 1919, the Stanley Cup was not awarded. Martin took the opportunity to represent Canada at the 2005 World Championship in Vienna, and the team almost ended the season in glory.

Canada advanced to the gold-medal game only to lose to the Czech Republic, 3-0. The game was difficult for Canada because only two top players—Rick Nash and Joe Thornton—had been playing in Europe all year whereas most of the Czech team had returned home to play. For Canada to have even won the silver medal was something of a minor miracle given the team's overall lack of training and conditioning.

After one year, the NHL was back for the 2005-06 season, and to try to make the game more interesting to fans in the United States who didn't know so much about hockey, the league introduced the shootout to make sure that all games

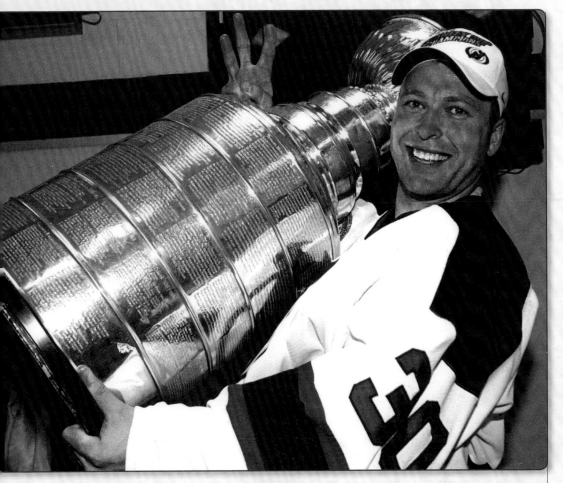

Martin has won three Stanley Cups during his career, and like all players who win, the trophy produces a great smile every time.

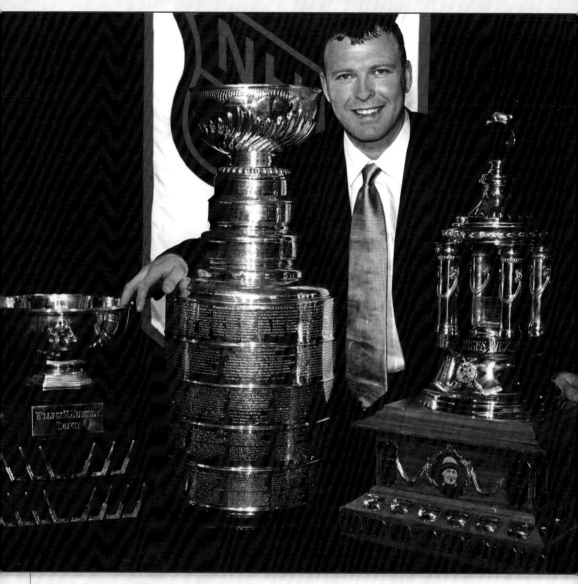

In 2002-03, Martin won the Stanley Cup with the Devils as well as two individual honours, the Jennings Trophy (left) and the Vézina Trophy.

had a clear winner and loser. Martin never liked the rule, and for good reason. He had played in many great and exciting games even though they ended in a tie. He also reasoned that a goalie's record could never again be compared to goalies of the past.

Still, Martin had to play within the rules, and he became one of the best shootout goalies in the league. Imagine how difficult it is to score on him with five opponents on the ice moving the puck around quickly. Now imagine only one opponent with the puck, clearly moving in from centre to the goal. Martin had a clear advantage and won many more games than he lost under the new format.

Another league initiative after the lockout was to reduce the size of goaltender's equipment. Thanks to Patrick Roy, goalies started to wear sweaters many sizes larger than needed. They also bulked up on pads, shoulder pads, and virtually every other piece of equipment that would increase their coverage of the net. The league wanted to change that to take any advantage away from the netminders and see higher-scoring games, which would give the fans more to cheer about perhaps. The NHL also formed a competition committee which included players, and Martin was the only goalie chosen

> *Martin had a clear advantage and won many more games than he lost under the new format.*

for the role which would go a long way, hopefully, to making the game more exciting and wide open. After a little more than a year, though, Martin resigned his position because he didn't believe the committee had much relevance.

"I didn't feel I was making a difference," he admitted. "I hate wasting my time when it doesn't seem to matter. I brought up a lot of different points...but nothing's changed...It's hard when nothing's improving and your name is associated with it. I didn't want to live with that."

CHASING RECORDS

CHAPTER EIGHT

"I love playing this game, and I want to play as hard as I can every night."

Martin

Being a goalie, Martin has his own personality and that is reflected in many aspects of his game. For instance, the made-up word JAWA is important to him because each letter represents the first letter of his four kids' names—Jeremy, Anthony, William, and Anabelle. Jeremy and William are twins. "JAWA" is painted on the back of his goalie mask.

Martin may be the best goalie in the world, but like most goalies he has his superstitions and quirky habits. Every game day Martin eats spaghetti to give him extra energy, and he arrives at the rink about two and a half hours before game time. He uses a new stick every game and writes the date of the game and the opposing team on the shaft to record the history of that night. When he gets dressed he always dons the left side first, then the right (i.e., left pad, right pad; left skate, right skate).

By the time Hockey Canada had to make its decisions for the 2006 Olympic Winter Games in Turin, Italy, Martin was playing as well as he ever had. He was named Canada's number-one goalie, and Roberto Luongo was made his backup. Just think what Martin had accomplished in the previous four years. He led Canada to Olympic gold in 2002. He took the New Jersey Devils to their third Stanley Cup win in the spring of 2003. He led Canada to victory in the 2004 World Cup of Hockey. He won the Vézina Trophy and Jennings Trophy in both 2003 and 2004.

Being named to the team was doubly important to Martin because of where the 2006 Games would be played. Remember his father, Denis, had played for Canada at the 1956 Olympics

◀ *Martin is deked by a Montreal player but rather than give up on the play Martin slides across the crease while blocking as much of the net as possible.*

the last time Italy hosted the Games, in a tiny town called Cortina d'Ampezzo. And now Martin had the chance to go to the same country, play for the same team, play the same position, and try to win gold for Canada. In fact, Martin had a special mask made for the 2006 Olympics. At the bottom was written Turin/Torino 2006, and on one side was Cortina d'Ampezzo 1956 and the other was Salt Lake City 2002 to honour the current tournament and previous appearances by his dad and himself.

Unfortunately, things didn't work out so well for the Canadians this year. Although Wayne Gretzky was in charge of the team and Pat Quinn was the coach—just as in 2002—the team chemistry wasn't quite the same. Still, Canada won its first game easily, 7-2 over Italy. Martin faced only 20 shots in this game, and in the next game, an easy 5-1 win over Germany, Roberto faced only 12 shots.

Canada was stunned in its next game, losing to Switzerland for the first time in Olympic competition by a 2-0 score. Martin played well, but there were two other stories that led to this result. First, both Swiss goals were scored by a former Canadian, Paul DiPietro, who had been living for several years in his new country and so was allowed to play for "La Suisse."

Second, Canada could not beat Martin Gerber in the Swiss net, despite sending 49 shots his way. Third, Rick Nash was denied a goal when Gerber made a glove save after the puck had crossed the goal line. Video review did not show the shot as a goal, but the next day, photographers showed they captured the save from the correct angle, and the puck was over the red line!

Canada lost the next game as well by the same 2-0 score, to Finland, but this time Roberto was in goal again. The team rebounded for a big 3-2 win over the Czechs, and it was Martin's great play that helped preserve the win. He made a sensational glove save off a one-timed shot from Jaromir Jagr in

The back of Martin's mask includes the initials of his four children, the A (far left) and A, J, and W representing Anthony, Jeremy, William, and Anabelle.

Viktor Kozlov of Russia brings the puck out front as Martin hugs the post during the quarter-finals of the 2006 Olympics in Turin.

the second period, and in the final 20 minutes when the Czechs held a 12-2 shots advantage, Martin was the difference between a win and a loss.

This set up a quarter-finals matchup against Russia. The preliminary round games didn't mean anything now, and both teams knew the winner would advance and the loser would go home. Of course, one of the keys to the game would be goaltending. Martin was in net for Canada, and Evgeni Nabokov for Russia. The game was tense and exciting for the first two periods, but it was still without a goal when teams came on the ice to start the third period.

The game turned in the first minute, though, when Todd Bertuzzi took a penalty, and with Canada down a man Alexander Ovechkin scored from in close after taking a pass from Viktor Kozlov behind the goal. Martin had no chance on the play, and the Russians added a second goal in the final minute to win, 2-0. Canada was going home.

Martin was especially discouraged by the loss, but he returned to New Jersey and tried to get back on the winning track with the Devils. Just before the Olympics he had signed a six-year contract extension with the team, meaning he would almost certainly retire having played his entire career with just one team, a rarity for a goalie in the game's history.

> *If there is any word to sum up the career of Martin, it is "consistent," and consistent at the highest level.*

If there is any word to sum up the career of Martin, it is "consistent," and consistent at the highest level. After the Olympics, he showed this quality again, and by the end of the season he had posted his usual amazing statistics. He appeared in 73 of the team's 82 games. He led the league with 43 wins. He had a goals-against average of 2.57. And, he took the team back to the playoffs.

This year the Devils faced geographic rivals New York Rangers in the first round, a matchup that hadn't occurred in nine years. Martin was at his best, and so were the players in front of him, and the Devils cruised to a four-game sweep of the Rangers. The last of the four games represented Martin's 137th consecutive playoff start, a new all-time record for goalies, surpassing Patrick Roy.

But the next round of the playoffs wasn't as successful. The Devils faced the Carolina Hurricanes, a younger, faster, hungrier team, and New Jersey had trouble containing their attack. The 'Canes won the series four games to one, and Martin and the Devils' season was over.

Because Martin is such a fierce competitor, losing any time, anywhere is a very frustrating feeling for him. But the NHL has 30 teams and so many great players that the reality is that Martin can't always win the big game or win the Stanley Cup. But although he didn't win the next year either, 2006-07, he did have perhaps the finest year of his career, even though he was now 34 years old and in his 14th NHL season.

> *Martin also won 40 games in a season for the sixth time during his career, extending his own record.*

Martin led the league by appearing in 78 games, just one fewer than the all-time record set by Grant Fuhr with St. Louis in 1995-96. But again, it was his consistency that made this heavy schedule possible. He set a new NHL record by winning 48 games, one better than Bernie Parent with Philadelphia in 1973-74. Martin also led the league with 12 shutouts to bring his career total to 92, third all-time behind only Terry Sawchuk (103) and George Hainsworth (94). Martin also won 40 games in a season for the sixth time during his career, extending his own record. Amazingly, no other goalie has more than three 40-win seasons.

In 2007-08, Martin won the Vézina Trophy ▶ for the fourth time in five years.

Martin also played 4,696 total minutes, a personal best. In the playoffs, the Devils eliminated Tampa Bay in six games in the first round, but in the next round they fell to Ottawa in five games. Martin started every game for New Jersey, taking his consecutive-start streak to 153, another record that might never be equaled. At the end of the season, he was the clear winner of the Vézina Trophy as the best goalie. It was the third time he had won the prize, and deservedly so. It wasn't going to be the last.

By the time the 2007-08 season arrived, Martin knew that his career had only a few years left. He also knew he was approaching the most important milestones a goalie has ever achieved in the history of the NHL. The team, however, was going through an important change. General manager Lou Lamoriello had hired a new coach in the summer, Brent Sutter, and the team took a little time to adjust to the new coach's methods. Martin started the season with 494 career wins, so of course he wanted to get to 500 as quickly as possible so the record wouldn't be a distraction to the team.

At the end of the season, he was the clear winner of the Vézina Trophy as the best goalie.

But the Devils started slowly and it took Martin 15 games to win five games. He then lost his next three games when he was at 499 looking for 500, but on November 17, 2007, in Philadelphia, he finally managed the historic victory. The Devils won the game, 6-2, and afterwards, his teammates chanted "Go, Brodeur, go!" in the dressing room.

"It's definitely nice to get it over with," he said, relieved. "We've spent a lot of time talking about it this year. It's a great accomplishment. To be able to do it with the same organization says a lot about whom I play for."

◀ *Players gather around Martin after his first career NHL game and victory.*

His teammate, Zach Parise was just as happy for his goalie. "Everyone was pretty excited for Marty. It's pretty cool to be part of it when something like that does happen." Indeed, only one other player has ever won 500 games—Patrick Roy. And Patrick needed 993 games to get to 500 whereas Martin reached the milestone in just his 908th game. The win meant that Patrick's career win record of 551 was now well within reach for Martin.

By the end of the year, both he and the Devils had adjusted to coach Sutter and the team was back on track. Martin played in 77 games and won 44 times. He played in 4,635 minutes, second best in his career to the previous season. He recorded only four shutouts, however, but more important he maintained his high level of consistency. Those four shutouts gave him a career total of 118 combining the regular season (96) and playoffs (22), and this was a new all-time record. The previous best was 115 by Terry Sawchuk (103 regular season, 12 playoffs).

> "Everyone was pretty excited for Marty. It's pretty cool to be part of it when something like that does happen."

Perhaps most amazing about Martin's accomplishments is that they have all come with the same team. Believe it or not, in the history of the NHL, there have been only two retired goalies—TWO!—among those who have played at least ten years in the league who have played their entire career with just one team—Turk Broda with Toronto and Mike Richter with the New York Rangers.

In the 2008 playoffs Martin was part of a bizarre controversy. The Devils again played the Rangers in the first round of the playoffs, but the Rangers had Sean Avery on the team, a "superpest" who annoyed opposing players through nasty words and aggravating actions. In one game of the series, he stood in front of Martin during a Rangers power play and waved his stick in Martin's face, not even looking at the puck. Although

he didn't receive a penalty on the play, the league declared the next day that such actions would be subject to an interference penalty in the future.

The local arena where Martin played as a kid is now named Martin Brodeur Arena, and the lobby displays some of Martin's equipment over the years.

Still, the Rangers won the series in five games and Martin was not at his best. Martin was too experienced to allow one player to annoy him, but he would have to wait another summer to prove himself all over again. Nevertheless, he was given the Vézina Trophy for a fourth time at the NHL Awards ceremony, another accomplishment for the history books.

And so the 2008-09 season will prove to be the crowning glory of Martin's career from a personal standpoint. Looking back, he has won three Stanley Cups, an Olympic gold, a World Cup of Hockey title, and two silver medals at the World Championship. As a team player, he has done it all. But soon his individual accomplishments will take him to a new level of success. He is only 32 games away from reaching 1,000 for his career, only the second goalie after Patrick Roy to reach this plateau. He needs only 14 wins to surpass Patrick for all-time wins, and he needs seven shutouts to tie Terry Sawchuk's mark

of 103 for the regular season, a mark everyone thought was simply unreachable after the great Sawchuk retired in 1970.

The best thing is, this isn't Martin's last season. He wants to play a few more years, and he has proved he can handle as many games as the coach will give him. Martin started playing hockey as any four-year-old boy in Canada, but he has pursued his dream with a determination that cannot be defined or described.

What is most amazing about Martin's career is that he has never been challenged as the team's dominant goalie. And, he has never missed more than a few games because of injury. He is as resilient as he is skilled. The New Jersey Devils have placed literally all of their faith in him since 1995, and he has responded by playing at a world-class level ever since.

Of course he has his bad games, but almost every time he has a poor performance he comes back and plays brilliantly. Of course he lets in bad goals, but again every time it seems he makes a great save later in the game to keep the score close or to assure victory. The joke is that when a second goalie comes to New Jersey, he can count on playing in maybe ten games a year. Maybe. It's Martin's crease and his alone.

> By the time he retires, he might well be considered the greatest goalie in the history of hockey.

By the time he retires, he might well be considered the greatest goalie in the history of hockey, a title he has earned one game at a time, one win at a time, one shutout at a time. But the key to his success is something more personal, as he revealed after winning the Vézina Trophy in 2007: "For me, it's the passion for the game. That's the bottom line. I love playing this game, and I want to play as hard as I can every night, every year I play."

◀ *Focused and committed, Martin takes a break during a stop in play.*

MARTIN BRODEUR BY THE NUMBERS

Martin Brodeur
b. Montreal, Quebec, May 6, 1972
6'2" 210 lbs., catches left

Selected 20th overall by New Jersey at 1990 NHL Entry Draft

Quebec Major Junior Hockey League

Regular Season		GP	W-L-T	Mins	GA	SO	GAA
1989-90	St. Hyacinthe	42	23-12-2	2,333	156	0	4.01
1990-91	St. Hyacinthe	52	22-24-4	2,946	162	2	3.30
1991-92	St. Hyacinthe	48	27-16-4	2,846	161	2	3.39
Totals		142	72-52-10	8,125	479	4	3.54

Playoffs		GP	W-L	Mins	GA	SO	GAA
1989-90	St. Hyacinthe	12	5-7	678	46	0	4.07
1990-91	St. Hyacinthe	4	0-4	232	16	0	4.14
1991-92	St. Hyacinthe	5	2-3	317	14	0	2.65
Totals		21	7-14	1,227	76	0	3.72

QMJHL All-Rookie Team (1989-90), QMJHL 2nd All-Star Team (1991-92)

American Hockey League

Regular Season		GP	W-L-T	Mins	GA	SO	GAA
1992-93	Utica	32	14-13-5	1,952	131	0	4.03

Playoffs		GP	W-L	Mins	GA	SO	GAA
1992-93	Utica	4	1-3	258	18	0	4.19

International

		GP	W-L-T	Mins	GA	SO	GAA	Result
1996	WC / CAN	3	0-1-1	140:00	8	0	3.43	Silver
1996	WCH / CAN	2	0-0-1	60:02	4	0	4.00	2nd
2002	OL / CAN	5	4-0-1	300:00	9	0	1.80	Gold
2004	WCH / CAN	5	5-0-0	300:00	5	1	1.00	1st
2005	WC / CAN	7	5-0-2	418:36	20	0	2.87	Silver
2006	OL / CAN	4	2-0-2	238:40	8	0	2.01	7th

CAN=Canada; WC=World Championships; WCH=World Cup of Hockey; OL=Olympics

Martin makes another glove save, one of thousands he's made with that quick left hand.

National Hockey League

Regular Season		GP	W-L-T-OT	Mins	GA	SO	GAA
1991-92	New Jersey	4	2-1-0	179	10	0	3.35
1993-94	New Jersey	47	27-11-8	2,625	105	3	2.40
1994-95	New Jersey	40	19-11-6	2,184	89	3	2.45
1995-96	New Jersey	77	34-30-12	4,433	173	6	2.34
1996-97	New Jersey	67	37-14-13	3,838	120	10	1.88
1997-98	New Jersey	70	43-17-8	4,128	130	10	1.89
1998-99	New Jersey	70	39-21-10	4,239	162	4	2.29
1999-2000	New Jersey	72	43-20-8	4,312	161	6	2.24
2000-01	New Jersey	72	42-17-11	4,297	166	9	2.32
2001-02	New Jersey	73	38-26-9	4,347	156	4	2.15
2002-03	New Jersey	73	41-23-9	4,374	147	9	2.02
2003-04	New Jersey	75	38-26-11	4,555	154	11	2.03
2004-05	New Jersey		NO NHL SEASON				
2005-06	New Jersey	73	43-23-0-7	4,365	187	5	2.57
2006-07	New Jersey	78	48-23-0-7	4,696	171	12	2.18
2007-08	New Jersey	77	44-27-0-6	4,635	168	4	2.17
Totals	15 years	968	538-290-105-20	57,207	2,099	96	2.20

NHL All-Rookie Team (1993-94)

Calder Trophy (1993-94)

NHL 1st All-Star Team (2002-03, 2003-04)

NHL 2nd All-Star Team (1996-97, 1997-98, 2005-06)

William Jennings Trophy (1996-97—shared with Mike Dunham, 1997-98, 2003-04, and 2002-03—shared with Roman Cechmanek & Robert Esche)

Vézina Trophy (2002-03, 2003-04, 2006-07, 2007-08)

Played in NHL All-Star Game (1996, 1997, 1998, 1999, 2000, 2001, 2003, 2004, 2007)

National Hockey League

Playoffs		GP	W-L	Mins	GA	SO	GAA
1991-92	New Jersey	1	0-1	32	3	0	5.63
1993-94	New Jersey	17	8-9	1,171	38	1	1.95
1994-95	New Jersey	20	16-4	1,222	34	3	1.67
1995-96	New Jersey		DNQ				
1996-97	New Jersey	10	5-5	659	19	2	1.73
1997-98	New Jersey	6	2-4	366	12	0	1.97
1998-99	New Jersey	7	3-4	425	20	0	2.82
1999-2000	New Jersey	23	16-7	1,450	39	2	1.61
2000-01	New Jersey	25	15-10	1,505	52	4	2.07
2001-02	New Jersey	6	2-4	381	9	1	1.42
2002-03	New Jersey	24	16-8	1,491	41	7	1.65
2003-04	New Jersey	5	1-4	298	13	0	2.62
2004-05	New Jersey		NO NHL SEASON				
2005-06	New Jersey	9	5-4	533	20	1	2.25
2006-07	New Jersey	11	5-6	688	28	1	2.44
2007-08	New Jersey	5	1-4	300	16	0	3.19
Totals	15 years	169	95-74	10,520	344	22	1.96

There is no drink more enjoyable than one taken from the bowl atop the Stanley Cup—only winners are allowed the privilege and honour.

Denis and Martin Brodeur, father and son, photographer and NHL star.

ABOUT THE PHOTOGRAPHS

For most books about a hockey player or team the author goes to public archives or news services to get the photographs. Not so in the case of *The Unbeatable Martin Brodeur*. All photos in this book were taken by Martin's father, Denis, a professional photographer for the Montreal Canadiens for decades. It was in part Denis' passion for hockey as well as photography that had made his collection as impressive as it is. Indeed, it is fair to say that there isn't a hockey player in the world who has had his career as well documented in pictures as Martin. His dad took pictures the first time Martin put on a pair of skates. He was there every time Martin played road hockey as a kid, every time Martin tried out for a new team in a new league in Montreal. Denis was at Martin's first NHL game, all his important Stanley Cup games, the Olympics, and World Cup games, not only taking pictures of Martin playing but also in the dressing room, with teammates, relaxing at home. No news service could possibly have provided the quality, quantity, and rarity of Denis' photos of his famous goalie son.